James Legge

A guide to the examination of the urine

designed chiefly for the use of clinical clerks and students

James Legge

A guide to the examination of the urine
designed chiefly for the use of clinical clerks and students

ISBN/EAN: 9783742828927

Manufactured in Europe, USA, Canada, Australia, Japa

Cover: Foto ©Thomas Meinert / pixelio.de

Manufactured and distributed by brebook publishing software
(www.brebook.com)

James Legge

A guide to the examination of the urine

A GUIDE

EXAMINATION OF THE URINE.

*

A GUIDE

TO THE

EXAMINATION OF THE URINE

DESIGNED CHIEFLY

FOR THE USE OF CLINICAL CLERKS AND STUDENTS

BY

J. WICKHAM LEGG, M.D.

FELLOW OF THE ROYAL COLLEGE OF PHYSICIANS OF LONDON
DEMONSTRATOR OF MORBID ANATOMY IN SAINT BARTHOLOMEW'S HOSPITAL.

Fourth Edition.

PHILADELPHIA:

LINDSAY AND BLAKISTON.

M. DCCC. LXXVI.

INTRODUCTION.

THIS little work is intended to supply the clinical clerk and student of medicine with a concise guide to the recognition of the more important characters of the urine; and from its small size to serve as a companion at the bedside to the busy practitioner, who may be unable to consult the larger works on the subject. A plan for the examination of the urine, step by step, has been given, with an account of the method for ascertaining the nature of those alterations that most frequently occur in disease. An appendix has been added in which the manner of estimating the urea, chlorides, phosphates, sugar, &c., by volumetric or other rapid analysis has been described.

London, *September*, 1869.

ADVERTISEMENT TO THE FOURTH EDITION.

The fourth edition has been carefully revised. An account of Dr. Russell and Dr. Samuel West's method of estimating urea has been added to the appendix.

47 Green Street.

June 17, 1876.

A GUIDE

EXAMINATION OF THE URINE.

In order that the examination of the urine may be made on a definite plan, the following scheme, in which the most important clinical facts are directed to be ascertained, is recommended to the student. The order of examination that is here given should be followed, the details of each operation being described on the page stated at the end of each paragraph.

SCHEME FOR THE EXAMINATION OF THE URINE.

I. Observe the colour of the urine, its appearance, if clear, smoky, turbid, &c. (page 3.)

II. Ascertain the specific gravity, (page 6.)

III. Examine the reaction, whether acid, neutral, or alkaline, by means of litmus or turmeric paper, (page 9.)

IV. Test the urine for albumen, (page 11.) If albuminous, look with the microscope for— renal casts, (page 63.); pus corpuscles, (page 56.); red blood corpuscles, (page 58.)

V. Test the urine for sugar, (page 18.)

VI. If there be no albumen or sugar present, and no deposit, the urine need not be further examined, unless some special indication exist.

VII. But if any sediment (page 42.) be observed, it must be examined with the microscope : the following enumeration of the more common deposits may help the student :

Pink or reddish deposit, dissolved on heating test-tube—urate of soda, (page 47.)

White crystalline deposit, soluble in acetic acid—phosphates, (page 50.)

Hummocky white sharply defined cloud, insoluble in acetic acid—oxalate of lime, (page 49.)

White amorphous flocculent deposit—rendered ropy by alkalies—pus, (page 56.)

Brownish-red crystalline deposit—uric acid, (page 44.)

Red amorphous deposit—blood, (page 58.)

PHYSICAL EXAMINATION.

The physical examination of the urine is the application of the senses to its investigation without the employment of chemical or microscopical aids. The colour, translucency, odour, and consistence are the only characters which can be ascertained by this simple method of observation.

Colour. Urine is ordinarily of a reddish yellow colour; but it may be as colourless as water, or dark brown black like porter; a smoky tint is absolutely diagnostic of the presence of blood; a brownish green suggests the presence of the colouring matter of the bile. Many drugs, as rhubarb, saffron, and santonin, give a peculiar red colour to the urine. The carbolic acid treatment of wounds colours the urine black. Tannin given by the mouth renders the urine colourless.

A pale urine is seen in health, as the *urina potus;* and in disease, in anæmia, diabetes, nervous disorders, and convalescence from acute diseases. A pale urine contains little colouring matter, and but a small proportion of solid constituents, always excepting, however, the urine of diabetes mellitus. A pale urine is a sign that the patient is not suffering any high degree of pyrexia. A high coloured urine occurs in health, after food as the *urina cibi*, and after strong exercise ; and in disease, in fevers, and most acute diseases, in which considerable metamorphosis of the tissues takes place. It contains much colouring matter and urea in proportion to the water. A dark urine should be examined for pigment. (See the section on pigment, page 30.) A dirty bluish coloured urine is sometimes seen in cholera and typhoid fever.

Translucency. In health, the urine deposits, after remaining at rest for a short time, a slight cloud of mucus, derived from the bladder and urinary passages; but, in all other respects, healthy urine is perfectly clear. On cooling, however, it may sometimes become turbid from the presence of urates, which are distinguished from other deposits by their appearing upon the cooling of urine which was perfectly clear when first passed. Should the urine be turbid when first voided, it is a mark of disease; and pus is the most frequent cause of this appearance.

Odour. It is not yet ascertained to what substance the peculiar smell of the urine is due, nor is it of much importance to the clinical student.

When the urine loses its **natural smell and be-**
comes fœtid and ammoniacal, the change is due to
the decomposition of urea into carbonate of am-
monia, and the formation of sulphur compounds;
in cases **of cystitis and paraplegia the alteration**
begins **very quickly after being voided. Various**
drugs, **as cubebs, and articles of diet as aspa-**
ragus, give a characteristic smell to the urine;
turpentine gives the odour of violets to the se-
cretion.

Consistence. **The urine is a limpid fluid, flow-**
ing freely from **one vessel to another. But in**
catarrh of the bladder, and in retention of urine,
the ammoniacal products of the decomposition of
the urea render the pus present thick and viscid,
thus causing **the secretion to be ropy, and poured**
with difficulty **from one vessel to another.**

The froth on normal urine readily disappears:
but if the froth be permanent, the presence of
albumen, **or of the constituents of the** bile, may
be suspected.

Before passing to the mechanical and **chemi-**
cal examination of the urine, **it may be well to**
mention the apparatus and reagents which will
be found necessary by the student for bedside
investigation. They are:

Cylindrical Urine Glasses, each containing about 6 fluid-ounces.

A Urometer, the stem of which is graduated from 1000 to 1060.

Blue and Red Litmus and Turmeric Paper.

Test Tubes.

A Spirit Lamp, or Bunsen's Gas-Burner.

Nitric Acid.

Acetic Acid.

Liquor Potassæ or Liquor Sodæ.

Solution of Sulphate of Copper, 10 grains to the fluid-ounce, or Fehling's Test Solution for Sugar.

Glass Funnel and Filtering Paper.

With this apparatus and these reagents, the student will be able to perform all the more important reactions described below.

SPECIFIC GRAVITY.

The specific gravity of the urine varies in health between 1015 and 1025; the simplest way of estimating it is by means of the urometer.

In order to use this instrument, a **quantity of**

the urine to be examined is poured into a cylindrical glass, and care is taken to remove all the froth which may form, either by blotting paper, or by overfilling the vessel. The urometer must then be slowly introduced, and allowed to float freely in the urine, without touching either the side or bottom of the vessel. Since the fluid accumulates around the stem of the urometer from the physical force of attraction, the specific gravity appears to be higher than it really is, when read off while the eye is above the surface of the fluid; to obtain a correct reading, therefore, the eye must be lowered to the level of the surface of the fluid, and the number on the stem ascertained by looking at it through the urine: having noted this, the urometer should be depressed in the urine, and again allowed to come to rest, when the number may be again read off; the second estimation is made to correct any mistake that may have taken place in the first reading. The specific gravity thus ascertained should be noted down at once. The urine must be of the temperature of the surrounding air, otherwise great errors may creep in.

The knowledge of the specific gravity of a

few ounces of urine is a matter of little value. To render the observation in any way service- able, the whole quantity passed in the 24 hours must be collected and mixed, and the specific gravity of a small amount of this taken. A rough estimation of the solid matters passed may be made from the specific gravity in the following way; the two last figures are multi- plied by 2 or 2·33 which gives the amount of solid matters in a 1000 parts of urine; if, for example the specific gravity of the urine be 1020, 1000 grains of urine will contain 2 × 20, *i.e.* 40 grains of solids, or multiplying by 2·33 = 46·6.

Clinical Import. Sugar in the urine is the most common cause of a high specific gravity; if this body be not present, excess of **urea** will be the probable cause.

A low specific gravity, below 1010, occurs after fluid has been taken in quantity. **A low specific gravity** is also noticed **frequently** in chronic Bright's disease, immediately after the paroxysm of hysteria, in anæmic states, and in diuresis from any cause, such as mental emotion, or exposure to cold.

A high specific gravity **with a** pale colour, **and a** low specific gravity with a deep **tint, are equally** signs of disease.

A new urometer should be carefully tested, since those sold by the instrument makers give results varying as much as 10 or 12 degrees. The urometers in common use in Hospitals are very rarely correct.

REACTION.

The urine is almost always secreted acid, although it may become alkaline within a very short time of being passed. In the majority of the cases in which the urine is said to be alkaline, as in paraplegia and cystitis, the alkalinity is really due to decomposition after being passed. If the urine, then, be found to be alkaline, a fresh specimen should be tested immediately after it has been voided. In cases of retention, the urine sometimes becomes alkaline in the bladder; and, in health, can be made alkaline, by the administration of drugs, such as the carbonates, acetates, citrates or tartrates of the alkalies.

When the alkalinity of the urine is due to ammonia, the brown colour of the turmeric disappears when the paper is exposed for some time to the air, or gently heated; but the change from yellow to brown is permanent, if the alkalinity be owing to either potash or soda.

The urine is rarely neutral to test paper; so that many observers have denied its occurrence. Occasionally the urine has an equivocal reaction, reddening blue litmus, and restoring the blue colour to reddened litmus paper. This amphigenous or amphoterous reaction, as it has been called, has not yet been satisfactorily explained; it is, however, without any clinical import.

The cause of the acid reaction of the urine is the presence of the acid phosphate of soda; and according to some observers, of free lactic and hippuric acids. Very shortly after being voided, the acidity increases, and lasts, in health, for days, free uric acid being often thrown down.

Sooner or later, however, the alkaline fermentation sets in, and the urine becomes ammoniacal and fœtid from the conversion of urea into carbonate of ammonia, and the formation of sulphide of ammonium, while the phosphates and the urate of ammonia are deposited as a white sediment.

Clinical Import. The acidity of the urine is decreased during digestion, and increased by fasting or perspiration. A very acid, high-coloured urine is associated with the "uric acid diathesis." This condition favours the occurrence of calculus and gravel.

Alkalinity of the urine is always due, if the administration of alkalies can be excluded, to the decomposition of urea into carbonate of ammonia. It is present in some diseases of the spinal chord, and especially in chronic affections of the bladder and urinary organs, as a few drops of urine, which have undergone the alkaline fermentation, will rapidly beget the same change in perfectly fresh urine.

When the alkalinity of the urine is due to fixed alkali, either potash or soda, it may be due to a catarrh of the urinary passages, the ingestion of alkaline salts, or some alteration in the metamorphosis of the tissues. About this last condition, little is known with certainty. It is always best treated by meat diet and iron.

EXAMINATION FOR ALBUMEN.

This is the first and most important step in the chemical examination of the urine: the presence or absence of albumen must always be determined before proceeding to test for any other substance, and the search must never be omitted in the examination of any urine. It is never present in natural urine.

The best way of testing for albumen is to fill a·test tube about two-thirds full of the urine to be examined, and to heat the upper layer of the fluid over the flame of a lamp, the lower end of the tube being held between the thumb and forefinger of the observer, in the manner represented in the accompanying wood cut. By employing this method, two strata of fluid are obtained for comparison.

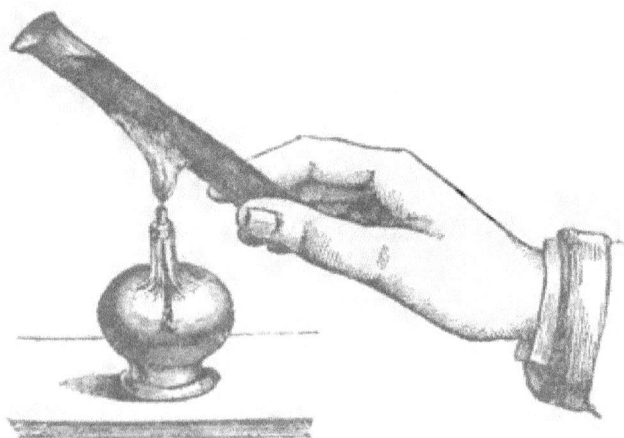

The heat is applied until the upper portion of the urine begins to boil, for although albumen

when in large quantity, coagulates at a point
many degrees below boiling, yet the presence of
a small quantity gives no precipitate below 212°
F. The boiled stratum of fluid should now be
carefully compared with the cool layer in the
lower part, by holding the test tube against the
light; if any cloudiness or opacity be seen, it
must not at once be concluded that albumen is
present; but a drop or two of dilute nitric acid
should be allowed to flow gently down the side
into the urine; the cloud is permanent, if due to
albumen; but disappears immediately if due to
the earthy phosphates. This addition of acid
after boiling should never be omitted, since the
most practised eye cannot distinguish, by appearance only, between the cloud produced by
albumen, and the phosphate of lime.

Cautions. i. The addition of the nitric acid
not unfrequently carries down some of the co-
agulated albumen into the unboiled layer of
urine, and thus causes the cloud to be less thick
than before; such an appearance is never produced by phosphates; when they are the cause
of the turbidity, the urine becomes absolutely
clear, as before boiling; slight brown colora-
tion only, occurring from the addition of the
nitric acid.

ii. Should the urine be turbid from the presence of urates, it quickly becomes clear on the application of slight heat; and as it is desirable before testing for albumen to have a clear solution, the whole of the test tube should be passed two or three times through the flame of the lamp, until the urates be dissolved; the upper stratum of the urine should then be boiled, and compared with the lower, as above.

iii. If the urine be neutral or alkaline at the time of testing, the albumen will not be precipitated by heat; the acid reaction must therefore be restored by a few drops of weak acetic acid, and the urine then boiled, and nitric acid added. If alkaline urine be boiled without previous acidulation, a deposit of phosphate of lime is almost sure to occur, which is immediately dissolved on the addition of an acid.

If nitric acid be added, before boiling, to an albuminous urine, the albumen will often not be precipitated on the application of heat. Care must therefore be taken that it is acetic acid which is used in the preparatory acidification of the urine.

iv. If the urine be permanently turbid, from any cause, and it is desired to know accurately whether albumen be present, the urine must be filtered before boiling; in this way very minute quantities may be discovered.

The method of testing for albumen, proposed by Heller, which consists in pouring nitric acid into a test tube, and allowing the urine to flow down upon the acid, so that the two fluids touch, but do not mix, and observing the layer of co-agulated albumen thus produced, is open to so many fallacies, that it cannot be recommended, save to experienced hands. Urea and urates are a common source of error, since they cause the appearance of a band very like that of albumen.

It is sometimes desirable to examine the urine for traces of albumen, and also for the presence or absence of substances very closely allied to albumen, but which cannot be detected by the usual tests for albumen. In this case the method recommended by · Millon should be followed. An equal weight of mercury is digested in an equal weight of strong nitric acid, first in the cold, and then by a gentle heat, until the metal be completely dissolved. Two volumes of water are then added to one volume of the mercurial solution. The whole is set aside for some hours, a crystalline deposit takes place, and the clear fluid is used for testing. This fluid colours red all solutions which contain a trace of an albuminous compound; the reaction appears in the cold, but is increased by warming up to near boiling point.

A rough way of estimating the amount of albumen present in the urine, is to pour some of the urine into a test tube, until it be about half full, and to boil the whole of the urine in the tube, till the albumen be completely coagulated. One or two drops of nitric acid are then added, and the test tube is set aside for 24 hours; at the end of that time, the proportion of the coagulated albumen, which has collected at the bottom of the tube, to the rest of the fluid, is noticed; if the albumen occupy one-third of the height of the fluid, there is said to be one-third of albumen in the urine; or one-sixth, or one-eighth, as may be. If, however, at the end of 24 hours scarcely any albumen have collected at the bottom, there is said to be a trace. If the urates have been deposited, the urine must be filtered before boiling, or a considerable error will creep in, by their increasing the apparent amount of albumen.

Clinical Import. The presence of albumen in urine is an important objective sign of disease.

Any state, which brings about a mechanical impediment to the return of blood from the kidneys, will be accompanied by albumen in the urine; and the albumen will be persistent so long as the congestion of the kidney continues; the longer the albumen remains in the urine, the greater danger is there of permanent textural injury to the kidney. In many acute febrile diseases, albumen is frequently present, which, as a rule, disappears with the termination of the illness; but, if persistent, it affords evidence of organic disease of the kidney. In a chronic, non-febrile disorder, without obvious impediment to the return of blood from the kidneys to the heart, the discovery of albumen in a clear urine would indicate structural change in the kidney.

The search for renal casts must always follow the detection of albumen in the urine. The discovery of these structures renders it certain that the albumen, or, at least, part of it, is derived from the kidney.

A common cause of the presence of albumen is pus, according to its quantity; in the urine of women, a small quantity of albumen is frequently due to leucorrhœal discharge, which is composed chiefly of pus. Gleet, and also, it is said, a great quantity of semen, cause albumen to be present in the urine.

If blood be present in the urine, albumen must likewise be present, derived from the corpuscles and plasma.

EXAMINATION FOR SUGAR.

If the specific gravity rise above 1030, sugar may be suspected, and should be looked for.

Many methods of testing for sugar have been proposed; but only the most prominent and trustworthy will here be mentioned, although it must be confessed that a rapid, and yet trustworthy, test, suited to practitioners, is still wanted.

Moore's Test. Equal parts of urine, and liquor potassæ or liquor sodæ, are poured into a test-tube, and the upper layer of this mixture is heated to boiling, in the manner described in the section on examination for albumen. (See page 12.) The heated portion becomes brown-red, dark-brown, or black, according to the quantity of sugar present. The least change of colour may be perceived by comparing the upper and the lower layers of the liquid.

Cautions. i. High coloured urines, and urines containing excess of phosphates, darken very perceptibly on boiling with caustic alkalies, and, if the urine be albuminous, the colour will be greatly deepened, though no sugar be present. Before, therefore, applying Moore's test to an albuminous urine; the albumen must be removed by filtration after boiling with a drop or two of acetic acid.

ii. It has been noticed that liquor potassæ which has been kept for a few weeks only in white glass bottles, takes up lead from the glass, and that a black precipitate of sulphide of lead is formed, when the alkali is boiled with certain urines which contain much sulphur. Care must be therefore taken that the liquor potassæ is free from lead.

The value of Moore's test is chiefly negative; if the urine on boiling with liquor potassæ do not greatly darken, it may be assumed to be free from a hurtful quantity of sugar; if, however, much darkening occur, a further observation must be made with the copper or fermentation tests described below.

The Copper Test depends on the property which grape sugar possesses, of reducing the higher oxyde of copper to a suboxyde. There are two methods of conducting this reaction, identical in principle, named respectively Trommer's Test. and Fehling's Test.

Trommer's Test. About a drachm of the suspected urine is poured into a test tube, and liquor potassæ, or liquor sodæ added in about the same quantity : a weak solution of sulphate of copper (about 10 grains to the fluid ounce) is dropped into the mixture. The precipitate which first forms is redissolved on shaking the test tube, and the copper solution should be carefully added, shaking the test tube after each drop has fallen into the mixture, so long as the precipitate is easily redissolved, when the solution will have acquired a beautiful blue or green colour, but should be quite clear, and free from any precipitate ; the contents of the test tube must next be heated to boiling, when, if sugar be present, an orange-red precipitate is first thrown down, which, after some time, becomes reddish brown. This precipitate consists of the suboxyde of copper.

Since uric acid and mucus will also reduce copper when they are boiled with its salts, a similar solution should be set aside in the cold ;

and if at the end of 24 hours the reddish precipitate have fallen, sugar is undoubtedly present.

Cautions. Much trouble is often at first felt in
arranging the proper proportion between the
copper solution, and the liquor potassæ. Much
of this, no doubt, arises from the weak pharma-
ceutical liquor potassæ being used instead of the
stronger solution of the chemical laboratory.
The liquor potassæ used in Trommer's test,
should be from 20 to 30 per cent. of strength.
This readily dissolves the precipitate formed on
adding the copper; a property which the phar-
maceutical solution possesses in much smaller
degree. Too much copper should not be added.
It is a good rule always to have a slight excess
of potash and never to operate save with a
clear solution.

Fehling's Test. In consequence of the difficulty
of properly adjusting the quantity of alkali and
copper in Trommer's test, many practitioners
prefer to use a solution in which the copper and
alkali are present in the exact proportion necessary. This solution may be prepared in the
following way: 665½ grains of crystallized
potassio-tartrate of soda are dissolved in 5
fluid ounces of a solution of caustic potash, sp.

gr. 1·12.   Into this alkaline solution is poured a
fluid prepared by dissolving 133½ grains of sulphate of copper in 10 fluid drachms of water.
The solution is exceedingly apt to decompose,
and must always be kept in stoppered bottles,
and in a cool place.   It is usually, therefore,
more convenient not to mix the alkali and copper
until the solution be wanted for use.   In this
case, a fluid drachm of the sulphate of copper
solution may be added to half a fluid ounce of
the alkaline solution prepared as above.

About a couple of drachms of this test-solution
are poured into an ordinary test-tube, and the
fluid boiled over a lamp.   If no deposit form, the
solution may be used for analysis; but if a red
precipitate be thrown down, the liquid has decomposed, and a fresh supply must be had.

While the solution is boiling in the test-tube,
the urine must be added to it drop by drop, and
the effect watched.   A few drops of urine which
contain a large percentage of sugar will at once
give a precipitate of yellow or red suboxyde; but
if no precipitate occur, the urine should be added
to the fluid, drop by drop, any deposit being
carefully looked for, until a quantity equal to

that of the Fehling's solution employed, have
been added.   If no precipitate be found after
setting the test-tube aside for an hour, the urine
may be considered free from sugar.

Cautions.   i.   The test solution should never
be used without boiling beforehand for a few
seconds ; the tartrate being exceedingly apt to
decompose, and the solution then reduces copper
as effectually as would grape sugar.

ii.   The quantity of urine used in the test
should never be greater than the quantity of
test-solution employed.

iii.   After adding urine in volume equal to the
Fehling's solution, the boiling of the mixture
must not be continued, as other bodies, besides
sugar, present in the urine, will reduce copper
at a high temperature.

Fermentation Test.   A few grains of German
yeast are put into a test-tube, which must then
be filled with urine, and inverted in a shallow
dish already containing a little of the urine, or
better still, quicksilver, and set aside in a warm
place, as a mantel piece, or a hob. A glass bird
fountain, if at hand, will be much more handy
for this purpose than a test-tube. A similar test-
tube or bird fountain must be filled with water,

a few grains of yeast added, and both vessels subjected to the same conditions. If sugar be present, the formation of carbonic acid will, at at the end of 24 hours, have driven nearly all the urine out of the test-tube or bird fountain, a few bubbles only will have appeared in that containing the water. To prove that this gas is carbonic acid, some caustic potash or soda must be introduced into the test-tube, when the gas will be quickly absorbed, and the urine again rise in the tube.

Estimation by loss of density after fermentation. Dr. Roberts has found that, after fermentation, "the number of degrees of 'density lost' indicated as many grains of sugar per fluid ounce," and he proposes to estimate by this means the amount of sugar present.

About 4 fluid ounces of the urine are placed in a 12-ounce bottle with a piece of German yeast of the size of a chestnut. The bottle is then set aside, very lightly covered, in a warm place, such as the mantel-piece, or hob, and by its side, a bottle filled with the same urine, but without any yeast, and tightly corked. In 24 hours the fermentation is almost finished ; the fermented urine is poured into a urine glass, and the specific gravity taken with the urometer; the specific gravity of the unfermented urine is also taken, and the specific gravity of the fermented is subtracted from the specific gravity of the unfermented, the remainder giving the number of grains of sugar contained in a fluid ounce: for example, if the specific gravity of the unfermented be 1040, and that of the fermented 1010, the number of grains of sugar in a fluid ounce will be 30.

According to Brücke, healthy urine contains sugar in about ·01 per cent. Consequently a healthy man excretes daily through the kidneys about 15 grains of sugar. According to Leube, the excretion of sugar in diabetes is far greater during the night, than during the day : urea follows just the opposite rule.

Clinical Import. If the foregoing tests announce the presence of sugar, in considerable quantity, as often as the urine is examined, diabetes mellitus may be inferred to exist. But should the presence of sugar in the urine be variable, and its amount small, the fact is not of any known great diagnostic, or therapeutic, importance.

Sugar is said to be present in the urine of the

fœtus, of women when suckling, and of some old persons. It is seen in the urine during convalescence from some acute disorders, especially cholera, in malarious diseases, and in carbuncle. Certain injuries of the nervous system also bring on glycosuria.

BILE IN THE URINE.

The presence of bile in the urine can seldom be overlooked, since it gives a dark greenish brown colour to the secretion. White filtering paper is coloured yellow by the urine; a permanent froth is also formed by shaking the urine.

Two bodies must be tested for, the bile pigments, and the bile acids, each of which must be looked for by itself.

The bile pigments. *Gmelin's Test.* Ordinary nitric acid, which nearly always contains some nitrous acid, is poured into a test-tube to the depth of half an inch. A portion of the urine to be examined is then gently poured down the side of the tube, held almost horizontally, on to the surface of the acid, so that the two fluids may touch but not mix; this operation is most con-

veniently performed by means of a **pipette. At
the line** of contact, **a zone of red appears in
every** urine; but **if pigment be present, a zone
above** becomes first green, **then violet, blue, and**
red, representing the **various stages of oxydation**
of the colouring **matters. The most characteristic
is the green; without it the presence of bile pigments cannot be predicated. This reaction** may
also be performed by allowing a drop of nitric
**acid, and of the urine to be examined, to run to-
gether on** a porcelain **dish, when the play of
colours** mentioned **above will be observed at
their line** of contact.

Caution. Any urine which contains a large
amount of indican will give a blue or violet, **and
even** green, colour with nitric **acid. The green**
colour **is, however,** rarely **seen with any other
substance than bile pigment.**

The **bile acids.** *Pettenkofer's Test.* Some of
the fluid **containing the bile acids, is** placed in
a porcelain dish, **and a drop of saturated** solution of cane sugar added ; strong sulphuric acid
is then dropped into the mixture, taking care
that this acid is clearly in excess of the **amount
of bile acid present, that is, about the same** volume as the **fluid containing the bile acids. On**

applying heat (which must only be moderate) a beautiful cherry-red colour is produced, passing into a deep purple. The purple colour is the only reaction characteristic of the presence of bile acids.

Another, and perhaps a better, way of applying Pettenkofer's test is to pour the fluid containing the bile acids, into a test tube; sulphuric acid being then added, at first in small quantity to precipitate the bile acids, but afterwards in amount sufficient to redissolve them, which renders the mixture perceptibly hot to the hand. A drop of syrup may now be let fall into the liquid, which then shows a play of colours passing from pink to cherry red, and from red to purple.

Strassburg recommends that the test should be applied to urine in this fashion: a little cane sugar is added to the urine and dissolved; a a piece of filtering paper is dipped in the urine and then dried. When the paper is quite dry, a drop of concentrated sulphuric acid is let fall upon it by means of a glass rod, and after a quarter of a minute a beautiful violet colour appears. I have used this test, but not very successfully. I feel unable to recommend it to the clinical student.

Pettenkofer's test should never be applied directly to urine: the bile acids are never present in sufficient quantity to give the reaction, however modified, and the urine in jaundice frequently contains a small quantity of albumen which gives a reddish violet reaction with sugar and sulphuric acid, while the action of the acid upon the other constituents of the urine renders it impossible to be sure of the distinctive colours of Pettenkofer's test. If, therefore, it be very desirable to ascertain whether the bile acids be present in the urine, the method introduced by Hoppe must be employed for their separation; a long and somewhat complicated process, which can seldom be adopted by the clinical student.

With this object, the urine must be rendered faintly ammoniacal with caustic ammonia, and then diacetate of lead added, so long as a precipitate occur. The precipitate must be collected on a filter, and washed with distilled water; then boiled with alcohol over a water bath, and filtered while hot ; to the filtrate a few drops of potash or soda are to be added, and the solution evaporated to dryness over a water bath. The residue is again to be boiled with absolute alcohol over a water bath until but a little be left. This must be then **thrown into a** great excess of æther in a stoppered bottle, and after some time, the alkaline salts of the bile acids will crystallize out. In order to prove that these crystals are salts of the bile acids, they must be dissolved in **a little distilled water, and tested with Petten-** kofer's method, as directed above.

Clinical Import. The bile pigments and the bile acids are present in the urine in most cases of jaundice. In hot weather, the bile pigments may sometimes be detected, by means of Gmelin's test, in the urine of persons who are not jaun- **diced. Indeed some** believe that the bile pig- ments are always present in small amount in health, and the **same may be** said of the bile acids. The quantity of bile acids present in jaundice is scarcely ever ·02 per cent., if the estimations on record may be trusted.

OTHER COLOURING MATTERS IN THE URINE.

The bile pigments are undoubtedly very near akin to the colouring matters of the blood. Hæmoglobin may be known to be present either by finding red corpuscles in the urine (see section on Blood, page 58.) or by the employment of the spectrum analysis. If this latter be out of the student's reach, Heller's test, which does not, however, separate hæmoglobin from hæmatin, may be used. Liquor potassæ or liquor sodæ is added to the urine in a test-tube, until a pronounced alkaline reaction be obtained, the mixture heated to the boiling point, and set aside for some time. The precipitate of phosphates has a greenish to a reddish colour, when the urine contains hæmoglobin, methæmoglobin, or or hæmatin. The colour is due to the hæmatin, a product of the decomposition of hæmoglobin. Another and very delicate reaction is the guaiacum test. To the urine are added a few drops of tincture of guaiacum and next an æthereal solution of peroxyde of hydrogen. If blood be present, a fine sapphire blue colour is developed.

Clinical Import. Hæmoglobin appears in urine in which no red blood corpuscles can be detected, in most cases of jaundice, in poisoning by sulphuric acid, phosphorus, and arseniuretted hydrogen. Also in malignant cases of the acute specific diseases, and in scurvy, hæmoglobin may be found, without any corpuscles being detected.

But little is known about the colouring matters of the urine which have been named urohæmatin, uroxanthin, hæmaphæin, &c. Indican is a constant constituent of the urine, and by boiling with mineral acids, is decomposed into sugar, indigo red and indigo blue. With nitric acid, it imitates the reactions of the bile pigment (see p. 26.) Heller pours a few drachms of fuming hydrochloric acid into a beaker glass and then adds about 30 or 40 drops of the urine. The fluid becomes red, violet, or blue if much indican have been present. Heller attributes the reaction to the presence of uroxanthin.

Clinical Import. Much indican is said to be present in the urine in melanotic cancers: the presence of indican may be of help to the diagnosis when the cancer is situated in an internal organ, for example, the liver.

UREA.

The clinical student may sometimes wish to know if the urine contain urea, or if a given fluid be really urine, or some other secretion. The fluid is first to be tested for albumen, which, if present, must be removed by acidulation with two or three drops of acetic acid, raising the temperature of the fluid to the boiling point, and filtering. This filtrate is used for the subsequent operations of evaporation, &c. as stated below.

If the urine be free from albumen, some quantity, 2 or 3 fluid ounces, must be evaporated in a Berlin dish over a water bath, until the fluid have the consistence of syrup. A water bath is essential, because an open flame would decompose the urea. After the syrupy fluid has completely cooled, nitric acid, as free as possible from nitrous acid, is added drop by drop, so long as a precipitate is formed. An excess of nitric acid is desirable. Some of these crystals of nitrate of urea, removed with a glass rod and placed under the microscope, show flat rhombic or hexagonal plates closely united to one another. Sometimes only a few drops of the fluid can be had, and the student should then let a little fall on a glass slide, set it aside in a warm place such as a mantel piece, for the fluid to concentrate, then add some strong nitric acid,

and place the crystals under the microscope.
If the fluid contain urea, rhombic or hexagonal plates will be seen.

Clinical Import. Urea is the most important
constituent of the urine ; a healthy man excretes
from 300 to 500 grains in the 24 hours. Its
amount is increased in health by a high meat
diet, and decreased by purely vegetable food.
In some acute diseases, as pneumonia, typhoid
fever, and acute rheumatism, it is said to be
greatly increased owing to the excessive tissue-
metamorphosis; it may be present in such
quantity as to give a precipitate, without previous concentration, when the urine is acidulated
with nitric acid.   Dr. Samuel West has, however,
found in these diseases that though the percentage of urea be high, owing to the small amount
of urine passed, yet the total amount of urea is
in many cases below the standard of health.
In chronic diseases, especially those attended by
a cachexia, or in uræmia and chronic Bright's
disease the amount of urea is below the average.

URIC ACID.

Uric acid is a less oxydised stage of urea.   If an urate be injected into the veins of an animal, an equivalent amount of urea appears in the urine.   Uric acid is found in the urine of all carnivorous animals.   In that of reptiles it entirely replaces the urea in the urine.

To ascertain if the urine contain uric acid, it is necesary to acidulate about a fluid ounce of the urine with a fluid drachm of hydrochloric acid, or strong acetic acid, in a suitable glass vessel, an ordinary beaker being best, and to set it aside, covered with a glass plate, for 24 or 48 hours.   At the end of that time, if uric acid be present, reddish brown crystals will be seen attached to the sides and bottom of the glass, or floating on the surface of the fluid.   These crystals have the flat rhombic, oval, or hexagonal shape of uric acid;   they are soluble in alkalies, and give with nitric acid and ammonia the murexid test.   (See page 46.)

A healthy man excretes, on an average, about 7 or 8 grains of uric acid in the 24 hours.

Clinical Import.   The excretion of uric acid is usually increased *pari passu* with the urea in pyrexia, or acute rheumatism, and in chronic liver diseases. It is increased out of proportion to the urea in leucæmia. An excess of uric acid is observed after an attack of gout; it is often entirely absent from the urine immediately before the paroxysm, and may disappear for days when this disease has become chronic.

HIPPURIC ACID.

The method of preparing hippuric acid from human urine is troublesome, and will rarely be required to be used by the clinical student. Two or more pints of perfectly fresh urine are evaporated to a syrup in a water bath and then extracted with alcohol. The solution is filtered, the filtrate evaporated over a water bath until a small quantity be left; and to this, when quite cold, hydrochloric acid is added so long as crystals are formed.

The crystals of hippuric acid obtained in this manner, seen under a microscope, are long and needle-shaped prisms; they are distinguished from those of benzoic acid by their difficult solubility in æther.

Hippuric acid, when evaporated to dryness with nitric acid, in a porcelain crucible, over a lamp, and then further heated to redness, gives off a gas smelling like oil of bitter almonds. This reaction is common to benzoic and hippuric acids.

Clinical Import. Hippuric acid exists in small quantity in the urine in health: its amount is greatly increased by the eating of much fruit, and also by the ingestion of benzoic acid. The hippuric acid appears in the urine in quantity equivalent to the benzoic acid taken. Excluding these circumstances, hippuric acid is also found in quantity in the urine of fever patients, and may even be the cause of the acid reaction: the amount is also increased in diabetes and cholera.

Nothing is known of the importance of this acid in therapeutics or diagnosis. In health the amount varies from 7 to 15 grains in the 24 hours.

CHLORIDES.

Chlorides may be known to be present by the following test. To a fluid drachm of urine in a test-tube, a drop of nitric acid is added, and then a few drops of a solution of nitrate of silver ; if a trace of chloride be present, a cloudiness only will be given; but if any quantity, a white precipitate is thrown down, soluble in caustic ammonia, and reprecipitated thence by the addition of nitric acid in excess.

The nitric acid is added at first to prevent the precipitation of the phosphates with the chlorides.

A rough comparative idea of the quantity of chloride present may be made from day to day, by always taking the same quantity of urine, acidulating it in a test-tube with nitric acid, and adding a solution of nitrate of silver until no further precipitate is formed. The test-tube must then be set aside for 24 hours, and a note then taken of the proportion of the chloride of silver deposit, for comparison with other observations.

On an average, a healthy man secretes 250 grains of chloride of sodium in the 24 hours.

Clinical Import. During acute pneumonia acute rheumatism, and most other pyrexial diseases the chlorides diminish in quantity, or even disappear from the urine. Their reappearance in daily increasing quantity is a sign of the diminution of the intensity of the disease. The amount of chlorides apparently depends upon the digestive powers of the patient, even in chronic diseases.

PHOSPHATES.

The presence of phosphates in the urine may be ascertained by the following test. A fluid is prepared by adding a drop or two of caustic ammonia to a fluid drachm of a solution of sulphate of magnesia in a test-tube; hydrochloric acid is added until the precipitate caused by the ammonia be redissolved. Caustic ammonia is again added in excess, until the fluid be strongly ammoniacal. A fluid drachm of urine is now poured into another test-tube, and rendered ammoniacal with caustic ammonia; to this urine some of the prepared solution is added, and a precipitate of the ammoniaco-magnesian phosphate occurs at once, if the urine contain the ordinary amount of phosphates; but the precipitate forms slowly, if the phosphates are present in very small amount.

The quantity of phosphoric acid excreted by a healthy man in the 24 hours is about 50 grains.

Clinical Import. The amount of phosphoric acid in the urine is increased in diseases of the nervous centres, and of the bones, and after great mental application. Acute febrile diseases cause increase of the phosphoric acid from increased tissue-metamorphosis, while in Bright's disease and some forms of dyspepsia the quantity of the phosphates is diminished. Dr. Gee has pointed out that the phosphates diminish or disappear after the acme of the paroxysm in ague.

SULPHATES.

The sulphates are at once recognised by the addition to some of the urine, in a test tube, of a drop of hydrochloric acid, and afterwards of a few drops of a solution of chloride of barium; a white precipitate, insoluble in nitric acid, is thrown down.

The quantity of sulphuric acid excreted by a healthy man in the 24 hours is about 30 grains.

Clinical Import. The quantity of the sulphates

is increased by a full animal diet; **very little is known** for certain of their amount **in disease, and** that little is at **present of not much inportance.**

The following table of the amount of urinary constituents excreted by a grown up man in the 24 hours is compiled from Dr. Parkes' book on the urine:

Quantity	40 to 50 fluid ounces.
Total Solids	800 to 1000 grains.
Urea	350 to 600 grains.
Uric Acid	5 to 15 grains.
Chlorine	50 to 150 grains.
Phosphoric Acid . .	30 to 60 grains.
Sulphuric Acid . . .	20 to 60 grains.

In a healthy **man, the hourly** excretion of urine may vary from **20 to 200 C.C. In** general, it is from 50 to 70 C.C. when much drink is taken, and 40 to 60 C.C. when little is taken. 1 kilogramme of body-weight, therefore, excretes about 1 C.C. of **urine** every hour.

The urine is always diminished **in quantity** during **the height** of a pyrexial disease: a sign

of improvement is the increase in the quantity
of urine.   When a disease is about to prove
fatal, the quantity often sinks.   In diabetes and
interstitial nephritis, the quantity is increased;
and this is often the case when collections of fluid
in serous cavities are being absorbed.

URINARY SEDIMENTS.

When a urinary deposit is to be examined,
about 4 or 5 fluid ounces of the urine should be
collected in a tall narrow cylindrical glass, and
set aside for a few hours. Cylindrical glasses
have, in my own experience, succeeded better
than conical vessels, since the sloping sides
of the latter tend to cause the sediment to
collect on them, without falling to the bottom.
This is particularly the case with uric acid and
renal casts, especially if they be present in but
small quantity.

When the sediment has collected at the bottom,
the supernatant urine may be poured off, and a

drop of the sediment placed on a glass slide, for examination under the microscope.

In looking for renal casts, it is better to use only the very last drops which fall from the vessel, after the rest of the urine is poured away.

Directions for the Microscope. A drop of the fluid containing the deposit is placed in the centre of the glass slide, which must be absolutely clean, and the drop very gradually covered with a piece of thin glass, (seven-eighths of an inch square is the best size), so as to drive all the air before it, and to prevent any air bubbles being present under the glass. This is best accomplished by the aid of a needle, placing one edge of the thin glass upon the slide, and resting the other upon the needle, then inclining the needle gradually, until it be horizontal. All superfluous moisture around the glass cover must be carefully removed with a cloth, or with blotting paper. The slide is then ready to be placed under the microscope.

A quarter-inch object glass will be sufficient for the recognition of nearly all the sediments that the student will have to deal with. The tube of the microscope must be moved down until the object **glass is** about a quarter of an **inch distant from the slide;** the **light from** the mirror is now **thrown upon the slide at a point immediately under the object glass;** the observer should **then look through the microscope, placing the instrument with the coarse adjuster** in the focus which suits his **own** eyesight.

Sediments are either organised or unorganised. **To the** latter belong uric acid, urates, **oxalate of lime,** phosphates, cystin, &c. **To the former, pus, blood, mucus and epithelium, renal casts, fungi, and spermatozoa.**

UNORGANISED SEDIMENTS.

URIC ACID.

Uric Acid is only met with as a deposit in **very acid urine, and is usually** accompanied by a considerable **sediment of urates.** Owing to its peculiar appearance, **like cayenne** pepper, it can at once be recognised **by** the naked eye, never being deposited from the urine in colourless crystals.

When the sediment is examined under the microscope, the crystals are at once known to be uric acid by their reddish brown colour, all other crystalline deposits being transparent and colourless. If indeed, the student be in doubt as to the nature of a crystal, he will never be very wrong, if he judge it to be uric acid when there is a slight tinge of brown visible. The crystals, themselves, have numerous forms: they occur very commonly in rhomboidal, or long oval, plates with acute angles; these crystals are often united so as to form rosettes, or they may be rectangular, barrel shaped, or in hexagonal plates, with two parallel sides longer than the other four.

Uric Acid.

If the student be not quite sure of their nature, he should add to the specimen under the microscope, a little liquor potassæ or liquor sodæ, which will dissolve uric acid, if present; when dissolved by the alkali, it can be reprecipitated in hexagonal plates by the addition of hydrochloric or acetic acid.

Traces may also be detected by means of the murexid test; a small portion of the suspected sediment is placed in a porcelain dish, and a drop of nitric acid let fall upon it; the dish is then gently heated over a lamp until all the nitric acid be driven off, when, if uric acid be present, a beautiful red staining is seen; after cooling, a drop of caustic ammonia should be allowed to roll over the reddened spot, which then becomes purple; if liquor potassæ be used instead of ammonia, the colour will be violet. The test does not, however, distinguish uric acid from its salts.

Usually the uric acid is not free when the urine is voided, but it is precipitated by the increase of acidity which always occurs shortly after emission, This is especially the case in the urine of diabetes, where the whole of the uric acid present may be set free from this cause.

Clinical Import. The presence of free uric acid is no proof that uric acid is being excreted in excess; the only inference that can be made, is that the urine is extremely acid. But if free uric acid shews itself immediately after the urine has been passed, it is not improbable that a deposit may be taking place in the pelvis of the kidney, or the bladder: a state of considerable danger, since it may lay the foundation of a calculus; uric acid, and urate, calculi being the most common of all urinary concretions.

URATES.

This deposit is the most common and least important of all the urinary sediments. Any febrile state will lead to this deposit; even a greater amount of perspiration than usual, will be followed by urine that becomes turbid on cooling, merely as a result of a diminished secretion of water. Urine containing an excess of urates is never turbid when fresh passed; it is only when the urine has cooled, that the peculiar muddiness is observed. If the urine be gently warmed, the turbidity immediately disappears.

The urates differ in colour considerably, according to the amount of colouring matter in the urine, varying from white to pink or red. In young children the 'milky' urine, which alarms mothers, is due to a deposit of peculiarly white urates.

In the urine, uric acid is found combined with three bases: with soda, with ammonia, and with lime. The urate of soda is the most frequent of the three, and is usually seen under the microscope as an amorphous deposit; sometimes it forms round dark bodies with short spikes projecting from them. The urate of ammonia is rarer, and occurs in beautiful globular forms with spikes closely resembling the urate of soda, but of greater length. The urate of lime is very rare, and forms only an amorphous sediment. If any doubt be entertained as to the nature of these salts, it is necessary to add a drop of hydrochloric or strong acetic acid to the specimen, when crystals of uric acid will immediately be formed. These crystals are again dissolved by caustic soda or potash. If further evidence be required, the murexid test with nitric acid and ammonia (page 46) may be applied.

OXALATE OF LIME.

Oxalate of lime is sometimes deposited from the urine during the acid fermentation, or even later.

Oxalate of lime occurs as a urinary sediment in colourless octahedral crystals, having the so-called 'envelope' appearance which, when once seen, can hardly be mistaken for anything else. This deposit also occurs in colourless dumb bells.

Oxalate of lime is insoluble in acetic acid; by this it is distinguished from the phosphates: it is colourless and insoluble in alkalies, and thus differs from uric acid. It is, however, soluble in the mineral acids, as, for example, in hydrochloric acid.

Clinical Import. After urates, oxalate of lime is the most common unorganised urinary sediment; it is often seen in the urine of patients convalescent from acute diseases; and many writers state that it may always be found when there is lessened oxydation, as in bronchitis. The occasional presence of a few crystals of oxalate of lime is not of much importance. They are frequently seen in the urine after the

E

eating of fresh fruit and vegetables. When the deposit is constant, and in large quantity, the formation of the mulberry calculus may be feared. This sediment is said to be associated with a dyspeptic and hypochondriacal condition, sometimes termed the "oxalic acid diathesis."

A   B

Ammoniaco-Magnesian
Phosphate.

Oxalate of Lime.
a. Dumb Bells.
b. Octahedra.

PHOSPHATES.

The phosphates are only separated from very feebly acid, or alkaline urine; and they are always deposited when the urine undergoes the

alkaline fermentation. They consist of the ammoniaco-magnesian phosphate, and the phosphate of lime. Both are usually found together.

Under the microscope, the ammoniaco-magnesian phosphate appears in beautiful right
rhombic prisms, which disappear immediately
on the addition of acetic acid, and are thus
distinguished from the oxalate of lime, with
which an inexperienced observer might, perhaps, confound them.

The phosphate of lime chiefly occurs as an
amorphous deposit; it is insoluble in water, but
soluble in acetic acid; in feebly acid urines, it
appears to be held in solution by the carbonic
acid, so that it is precipitated by heat in flakes
resembling albumen, which are at once, however, dissolved by a drop of acid.

Clinical Import. The deposit of phosphates
indicates an alkaline reaction of the urine, a
condition favourable to the formation of phosphatic calculi.

If the least doubt be left upon the observer's
mind after the microscopical examination of a
sediment, he must use the aid of reagents in
determining its nature. The following scheme

will be found useful: a drop of strong acetic acid should be placed on the glass slide, near the thin covering glass, so that the acid may run in between the two pieces of glass, but it should be carefully prevented from wetting the upper surface of the cover, as this will produce an obscurity over the object. Or after having placed a drop of the fluid containing the sediment upon the glass slide, the end of a thread should be placed in the drop, and then the covering glass laid upon it, so that the other end remains free: the acid or other reagent may then be placed upon the free end of the thread, and is thus conducted along the thread to the sediment under the cover. Should the deposit be phosphatic, the acid quickly dissolves the crystals, or amorphous sediment; but if the sediment consists of urates, crystals possessing the well-known shape of uric acid are formed. If no effect upon the sediment is produced by acetic acid, it consists of either uric acid, or oxalate of lime. Liquor potassæ, added with the same precautions as acetic acid, brings about a solution of the crystals of uric acid, but the alkali has no effect upon the oxalate of lime, which will be dissolved by the action of hydrochloric acid.

CYSTIN.

Cystin is a rare deposit in the urine : it occurs in regular colourless hexagonal plates, united by their flat surfaces, and overlapping one another. When dissolved in the urine, cystin may be thrown down by the addition of acetic acid, and the precipitate examined under the microscope. It may be distinguished from uric acid, which sometimes crystallizes in hexagonal plates, by the absence of colour in the crystals.

Urine which contains cystin is usually feebly acid, of a yellowish green colour, and of a peculiar odour, compared to sweet briar, but which sometimes resembles that of putrid cabbage. The urea and uric acid are diminished in most cases. The ammoniaco-magnesian phosphate often accompanies the crystals of cystin.

Cystin contains a large quantity of sulphur, and Liebig proposed a test which is founded on this fact. A solution is made by adding to a small quantity of solution of acetate of lead liquor potassæ or liquor sodæ until the precipitate first formed be redissolved ; about equal parts of this solution and of urine are boiled, when black sulphide of lead is formed from the combination of the sulphur with the lead. This test is, however, by no means a good one, since many bodies frequently present in the urine, for example, albumen, contain enough sulphur to give the reaction.

Of the *Clinical Import*, nothing is known.

The appearance of cystin in the urine is believed by some to be hereditary and to be connected with calculous disorders. Other observers have found it in the urine of chlorosis.

LEUCIN AND TYROSIN.

Leucin and Tyrosin are very rare deposits in the urine. Under the microscope, leucin appears in dark globular forms, which have been compared to masses of fat cells; tyrosin, however, crystallizes in beautiful bundles of delicate needles, sometimes arranged in a stellate form.

These bodies have been detected in the urine in cases of acute yellow atrophy of the liver, of small pox, of typhoid fever, and acute tuberculosis.

If these bodies do not occur as a sediment they may be looked for by the following method a large quantity of the urine must have a solution of acetate of lead added to it so long as a precipitate forms. Through the filtrate sulphuretted hydrogen is passed to remove the excess of lead; and the fluid is filtered again, evaporated over a water bath to a syrup and then extracted with spirit. The leucin is dissolved in the spirit while the tyrosin for the greater part remains undissolved. The part insoluble in spirit may now be dissolved in water and boiled with a few drops of nitrate of mercury; if tyrosin be present, the fluid becomes rose red and soon after a red precipitate is thrown down. This test for tyrosin is called Hoffmann's test and is said to be very delicate.

The solution in spirit contains the impure leucin and requires further preparation. It must again be filtered, evaporated to dryness and dissolved in ammonia, and then acetate of lead added so long as a precipitate forms, then filtered and washed with a little water. The precipitate on the filter, which is a combination of leucin with lead, is suspended in water and sulphuretted hydrogen passed through, the liquid again filtered, evaporated and set aside to crys-. tallize. The crystals that form must be tested in the following manner. They are carefully heated with nitric acid in a platinum crucible: if leucin be present a colourless almost invisible residue is left which, warmed with a few drops of soda solution, becomes of a yellow colour passing into brown. Another test is this; if leucin be heated in a dry test-tube, oily drops are formed which give off the smell of amylamin.

This preparation is undoubtedly very long and troublesome; but without it, it is impossible to speak with confidence of the presence of leucin and tyrosin: of course, if a sediment suspected to be leucin or tyrosin be found in the urine it may be tested at once by the tests given above. But the recognition of crystals under the microscope having the same form as leucin and tyrosin, is of no value, as in many cases, whether in health or disease, urine will give crystals identical in form with leucin and tyrosin but in which the chemical tests altogether fail.

ORGANISED SEDIMENTS.

PUS.

Pus is often present in the urine, and forms a

thick sediment at the bottom of the urine glass. The urine readily becomes alkaline, and rapidly decomposes after being passed. It is permanently turbid; that is, the turbidity is unaffected by heat.

Under the microscope, the deposit shows numerous pus corpuscles, round colourless bodies, not varying much in size, having granular contents, and nuclei varying from 1 to 4 in number; if acted on by acetic acid, the nuclei become much more distinct. If the urine have been long passed, the pus corpuscles undergo changes which render them incapable of being recognised.

The urine of course contains albumen, and in proportion to the amount of pus present. If the quantity of albumen exceed that which should be given by the pus present in the urine, evidence of kidney disease, as casts of tubes, should at once be looked for.

The deposit from urine containing pus is rendered viscid and gelatinous by the addition of about half its quantity of liquor potassæ; it becomes ropy and cannot be dropped from one vessel to the other; urine containing mucus on the other hand, becomes more fluid and limpid by the addition of caustic alkali.

Pus occurs in the urine in the following diseases:

> Leucorrhœa in women.
> Gonorrhœa or Gleet in men.
> Pyelitis, from any cause.
> Cystitis.
> Any abscess bursting into any part of the urinary tract.

Leucorrhœa is an exceedingly frequent cause of the presence of a slight amount of albumen in the urine of women; if it be necessary to exclude this origin, the urine must be obtained by means of the catheter.

BLOOD.

Blood is not at all unfrequently found in the urine, and it may be derived from any part of the urinary-renal tract. If derived from the kidneys, the blood will be completely diffused through the urine, and give it a peculiar smoky appearance, quite diagnostic. If the hæmorrhage from the kidney be great, however, the urine will have a bright red colour, like blood. But when the urine contains a great deal of blood, the blood is usually derived, not from the kidneys, but from some other part of the urinary tract.

The deposit at the bottom of the urine glass shows under the microscope the circular discs, familiar to every one as the red corpuscles of the blood. Their peculiar colour will prevent the student mistaking them for any other deposit ; they may, however, in a urine of low specific gravity, become swollen, pale, and at last burst from endosmosis ; in those of high specific gravity, they will often become contracted, shrivelled, and distorted, from exosmosis.

The urine will, of course, contain albumen in proportion to the quantity of blood present, which may be so great that the urine will solidify on the application of heat. The urine very readily becomes alkaline, and care must be taken to restore the acid reaction with acetic acid, before testing for albumen.

Clinical Import. The presence of blood or of blood corpuscles, in the urine is a sign of hæmorrhage from the kidney or the urinary passages. It may result from:

   i. *Disease of the Kidney.*

      Acute Bright's disease.

    Congestion of kidney.

    Cancer of kidney.

    External injury.

ii. *Disease of Pelvis and Ureter.*

    Calculus in pelvis or ureter.

    Parasite, as Bilharzia hæmotobia.

    Cancer.

iii. *Disease of the Bladder.*

    Calculus.

    Cancerous or villous growths.

    Congestion or ulceration of mucous membrane.

iv. *Disease of Urethra.*

    Congestion, as in gonorrhœa.

    Tearing of the mucous membrane from mechanical injury.

v. In women, uterine discharges, as menstruation, &c.

If the amount of blood in the urine be small, the chances favour the belief that the blood is derived from the kidneys; search must therefore be made for renal casts. If the amount of blood be large, it probably comes from the pelvis of kidney, ureter, or bladder; if from the pelvis or ureter there will also be pus and probably also gravel in the urine, with pains in the loins, passing down into the thighs and testicles. If there be none of these indications, the blood probably comes from the bladder. It is commonly said, that if the blood be com- pletely mixed with the urine, the hæmorrhage is from the kidneys; if the urine first passed be clear, and that at the end of micturition, become bloody, or if even pure blood be passed, the hæmorrhage is from the bladder or prostate; while, if the first portion of the urine be bloody, and the last drops clear, the hæmorrhage is from the urethra. These rules will, however, often be found to fail.

The chief danger of hæmaturia is the forma- ·tion of clots in the. passages and consequent ischuria. Small clots may sometimes form the nucleus of a calculus.

MUCUS AND EPITHELIUM.

Mucus is a constant constituent of every urine, and if healthy urine be allowed to remain at rest for an hour, a light cloud will be found to have settled at the bottom of the urine glass; on examination with the microscope, it will be found to consist of mucus corpuscles, and epithelium scales detached from the surfaces over which the urine has passed.

The urethra and bladder give up a roundish or oval epithelium cell to the urine. In the urine of women, especially in cases of leucorrhœa, the epithelium cells of the vagina are very numerous; they exactly resemble the squamous epithelium of the mouth. Under irritation, the mucous membrane of the pelvis and ureter will produce cells, caudate, spindle-shaped, and irregular, very like to those formerly looked upon as diagnostic of cancer. From this circumstance it is impossible to speak positively of the existence of cancer cells in the urine.

Desquamation of the tubular epithelium of the kidney occurs only in disease ; the cells as seen in the urine, are slightly swollen, and acquire a more spheroidal, and less distinctly polygonal shape, apparently from the imbibition of fluid, and the removal of pressure. The cells are frequently granular, and contain fat drops, or are contracted, withered up, and shrivelled.

Clinical Import. See Section on Renal Casts. page 68.

RENAL CASTS.

In Bright's disease, and in congestion of the kidney, there are formed, in the uriniferous tubules, lengthened cylinders which are discharged with the urine, and form the deposit known as "casts." Those found in the urine are probably chiefly formed in the straight uriniferous tubes; and the view of their origin, which has found most favour in this country, is that the casts are formed by the escape of blood or plasma into the tubes of the kidney, and coagulation of the fibrin, which thus becomes moulded to the shape of the tube into which it has been extravasated. It is probable that many of the hyaline casts are formed in this way; but the balance of evidence at the present day is in favour of the epithelial and granular casts being produced by a desquamation and degeneration of the renal epithelium.

When the urine contains casts in great quantity, they can scarcely be overlooked, if the urine be allowed to settle for a few hours in a tall cylindrical glass the whole of the supernatant fluid poured off, and the last drops which flow from the lip of the glass put under the microscope and examined. If there be but few casts present, the whole of the urine of the 24 hours should be collected in a tall glass and allowed to settle for about 12 hours. The urine must then be all poured away, save the four or five ounces which have collected at the bottom. This residue must then be allowed to settle again for a few hours, when if casts be present, they will be found at the bottom of the glass, the last drops poured away being put under the microscope. Casts may oftentimes be missed if the urine given for examination be only the upper layer of a specimen which has settled for some time and of which all the casts have fallen to the bottom. It thus sometimes becomes of importance to collect all the urine passed.

With a little experience, the student will soon become familiar with the appearance of casts, and will at once be able to distinguish them from foreign bodies in the urine. They are never broader than 6, or less than 2, red blood corpuscles in diameter; but they vary considerably in length, never, however, exceeding the $\frac{1}{50}$th of an inch. The same cast does not vary greatly in

its diameter, and never becomes twisted on itself, as a cotton fibre does.

The foreign bodies, most liable to be mistaken
for renal casts, are cotton fibres, hair, and pieces
of deal.

Cotton fibres have a very irregular outline, and
are much broader at one point than at another;
they are often twisted, and of great length,
which will distinguish them from casts. Their
structure is often striped in a longitudinal direc-
tion.

Hair can often be distinguished from renal
casts by its colour alone; and if this be not very
apparent, by its possessing a cortical and medul-
lary structure; and by its length being greater
than that of any cast.

Fibres of Deal, which have their source in
furniture, flooring, &c., may perhaps be mistaken for renal casts. They are at once recognised by the presence of the large round wood-
cells which characterise the order of Coniferæ.

Casts may be conveniently divided, according
to their appearance under the microscope, into
three kinds, the epithelial cast, the granular cast,
and the hyaline cast.

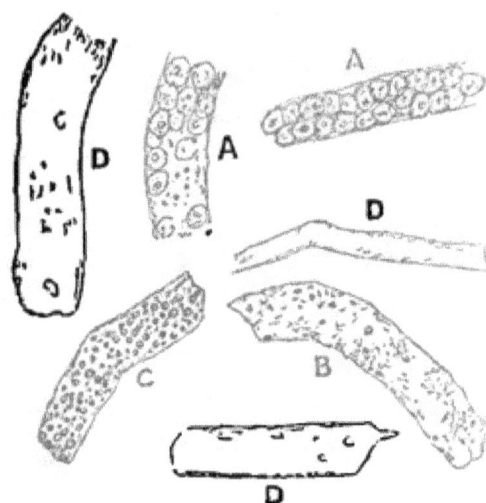

CASTS—A. Epithelial. B. Granular. C. Fatty. D. Hyaline.

The epithelial cast. This cylinder consists of
a mass of epithelium cells derived from the tubules of the kidney ; the cells may become granular and acquire a dark appearance by transmitted light. The cast is usually wide, never very
narrow.

The granular cast. This is a solid cylinder
having a granular appearance, which may be
limited to a few dark points in the substance
of the cast, or be so intense as to give the cast
an almost black appearance. In this kind of
cast may often be found epithelial cells, blood
corpuscles, red or white, pus corpuscles, crystals
of uric acid, urates, and especially oxalate of

lime. The fatty cast is a variety of the granular, produced by the running together into globules of the granules of fat.

The hyaline cast. This cast is usually very transparent, and the outline is often so indistinct that a little iodine or magenta must be added to the urine before it can be detected, or a diaphragm with a narrow opening must be used. They show indistinct markings on their surface, or a few granules and nuclei. There are two kinds, the wide and the narrow ; the latter are sometimes of great length.

In observing casts, notice must be taken of the action of acids upon them, or their contents. It is thought that when the cylinders resist the solvent action of hydrochloric acid to any great degree, that the inflammation of the kidney is correspondingly intense. The granules on the cast, if albuminous, will disappear, when acted on by acetic acid ; but if oily, they are rendered more distinct. The width of the cylinder is of some importance, as it is supposed that very broad casts are formed in tubules completely stripped of their epithelium, and that the prognosis is more grave when these wide casts show on their sides no nuclei, or attempt at re-formation of epithelium. From the recent observations on the varying diameters of the uriniferous tubes, the importance of the breadth of the cast becomes less.

Clinical Import. The presence of casts in the urine is a sure sign of disease of the kidney, but not, however, necessarily of permanent disease of the kidney. They are present in many acute diseases, accompanied by albumen in the urine; but if they are found for several weeks together, after all fever have left the patient, then permanent disease of the kidney may be inferred. Casts are constantly present in the urine in all cases of congestion of the kidney, and of acute or chronic Bright's disease. But no certain information as to the nature of the disease existing in the kidney, for example, whether lardaceous or otherwise, can be had from the characters of the casts, since all forms of Bright's disease end in fatty changes. Some help may, however, be derived from the appearance of the casts in forming a judgment of the acute or chronic character, or a prognosis, of the disease. If, for example, there be found in the urine epithelial casts which have undergone little, or no, granular change, and casts

studded with red blood-corpuscles, together **with**
a large quantity of epithelium from the tubules
of the kidney, **having a natural or** only slightly
clouded **appearance, there can be** little doubt
that the patient is **suffering from an acute attack
of Bright's disease : while if the casts be** chiefly
fatty, or intensely granular, and the epithelium
be small in amount, and the cells withered and
contracted, or containing globules of oil, it will
be more than probable that the case is one of
chronic Bright's **disease.**

Since little trust can be put **in the** characters
of the casts as an aid to special diagnosis, some
of the leading characters of the renal derivatives
in the chief forms of kidney affection **will now**
be spoken of more at length.

Congestion of the Kidney. **The casts are** chiefly
hyaline, seldom showing any marks of fatty
change. **Very rarely may blood or** epithelial
casts be discovered.

*Acute Bright's **disease.** **At the** beginning, the
urine deposits a sediment which consists of
blood-corpuscles, narrow hyaline casts, and casts
covered with blood-corpuscles, **the 'blood cast'
of some authors. In the next stage, the** amount
of blood **present is not so great, but, a great**

desquamation of the renal tubules taking place, renal epithelium and epithelial casts are found in great numbers; the epithelium has undergone little, if any, granular change; hyaline casts are observed together with epithelial. In the next stage, the changes in the epithelium may be almost daily observed; at first they become granular, cloudy in appearance, which change often goes on to fatty degeneration, and the epitheial cells then contain large fat drops, while the epithelial casts undergo a like change, and become distinctly granular and even fatty.

If the patient recover, the casts and epithelium slowly disappear from the urine, but if the case become chronic, the renal derivatives show the characters described in the next paragraph.

Chronic Bright's Disease. Numerous forms of casts are met with; the hyaline, both narrow and wide forms; the larger are often beset with granules dissolved on the addition of acetic acid; the granular, whose surface is often covered with fatty or shrivelled-up epithelium cells; fat drops may stud the cylinder. Epithelial casts are rare, except in febrile exacerbations, when the renal derivatives found in acute Bright's disease are present, together with granular and fatty casts, evidence of the previous alteration of the kidney.

Lardaceous or Amyloid Kidney. The urinary deposit contains hyaline casts, which are often accompanied by pus corpuscles. Atrophied epithelial cells, becoming fatty in the latter stages of the disease, are almost invariably present.

FUNGI.

Many kinds of fungi grow in the urine after it has been voided for some time, and when the ammoniacal decomposition has begun, or is about to begin. The most important are (*a*) *bacteria,* also known as *vibriones, monas crepusculum, microzyma* and the like. Their origin is now warmly contested, but it cannot yet be said that any source save that of *omne ovum ex ovo* has been proved. They will be often known by their incessant motion; but care must be taken not to confound with bacteria inorganic particles showing the molecular movement. They show various forms, chiefly linear, and need a high power of the microscope to recognise them; (*b*) the *penicilium glaucum,* the fungus which forms 'mildew,' and which often appears when the acid fermentation has begun; (c) the yeast fungus, *torula cerevisiæ*, or *saccharomyces urinæl*, oval cells about the size of a blood-corpuscle joined together in a row, considered by Dr. Hassall to be diagnostic of diabetes; *(d) sarcinæ* are apparently formed in the urine before it be voided; they are square bodies, divided into secondary squares, which number 4, 16, 64, &c., and are like the sarcinæ found in the vomited matters of persons suffering from stenosis of the pylorus.

Kiestein is a whitish pellicle formed on the surface of the urine of pregnant women, when allowed to remain at rest for a few days. It appears to consist chiefly of the mould fungus, globules of fat, and crystals of phosphates. Formerly it was thought to be a sign of pregnancy; but it is seen in the urine of men and it is not always present in pregnancy.

SPERMATOZOA.

These little bodies are present in the urine of men first passed after an emission of semen. A few pass away in the urine, probably, without venereal excitement, especially when the person is continent. In the urine of women, they are almost positive proof of sexual intercourse.

The seminal secretion forms a glairy white deposit at the bottom of the urine glass. When examined with the microscope, (for which a high power, magnifying 400 or 500 diameters, is best, although a power of 250 will identify them), spermatozoa show the characteristic oval head or body, often somewhat pear-shaped, and long delicate tail, two or three times the length of the head. In the urine no movement is ever shewn by these bodies.

APPENDIX.

It has been thought desirable to add a short account of the method of estimating the chief substances found in the urine, since the clinical clerk may often be desired to make an analysis of the urea, chlorides, phosphates, &c. No account of the method of making standard solutions will be given, as this preparation requires a greater knowledge of chemistry than is usually possessed by the clinical student. For the same reason, no details have been introduced which require the use of a balance.

The metric weights and measures only will be employed : they are

The litre, the unit for measures of capacity= 1·76 pints.

The cubic centimeter, (C.C.) the $\frac{1}{1000}$th part of a litre.

The gramme, (grm.) the unit of weight, the weight of a cubic centimeter of distilled water, at 4°C. at normal barometer pressure,=15·43 English grains.

The milligramme, the $\frac{1}{1000}$th part of a gramme.

The apparatus required will be :

A measure of litre capacity, divided into parts containing 10 C.C. at least.

Burettes, divided into quarters of a C.C.

Pipettes, which deliver 5, 10, 15, 20, 30 and 50 C.C.

Beakers, Berlin dishes, stirring rods, &c.

GENERAL DIRECTIONS.

The whole of the urine passed in the 24 hours must be obtained: it will be found most convenient to collect it from 9 a.m. on one day to 9 a.m. on the following day, making the patient micturate precisely at this hour.

The urine must be kept, as it is passed, in a covered glass vessel. When the analysis is to be made, the urine must be measured in a vessel graduated to a 1000 C.C., and divided into parts containing at least 10 C.C. each. After measuring, the whole of the urine must be mixed together, and a portion of this used in the estimation of the urea, chlorides, &c.

A complication arises if the urine contain albumen; and, in this case, the albumen must be removed before proceeding to the analysis of the urea, &c.; a measured quantity of urine, 100 or 200 C.C. is heated in a Berlin dish, the bottom of which is protected by a piece of iron wire gauze, over a small, naked flame, to nearly the boiling point. If the albumen do not separate in flakes, dilute acetic acid is *very* carefully added until the acid reaction be marked. If too much acetic acid be added, part of the albumen may be redissolved. The heat must be moderate, and only just rise to boiling point, or the urea will be decomposed. The urine, after cooling, is then to be filtered into the same measure that was used at the beginning to ascertain the volume (100 or 200 C.C.), the dish and filter washed with small quantities of distilled water, which are added to the filtrate, until the urine stand at exactly 100 or 200 C.C. according to the initial quantity. This fluid is then used in the estimation of the urea, chlorides, phosphates, sugar, &c.

ESTIMATION OF UREA.

There are two methods now commonly in use for the estimation of urea: one, lately introduced by Dr. Russell and Dr. Samuel West; the other, a method first employed by Liebig and known by his name.

In both of these it is necessary to ascertain beforehand the presence or absence of albumen. If albumen be present, it must be separated by the method given on the page above. If the urine be free from albumen, both the methods may be used without further preparation of the urine.

The first process, a modification of Hüfner's, is based upon the fact that when urea is acted on by an alkaline hypobromite, nitrogen is given off, and this nitrogen, when collected and measured, gives an estimation of the urea decomposed.

The hypobromite solution used in this process is made by dissolving 100 grammes of common solid caustic soda in 250 C.C. of water and then gradually adding 25 C.C. of bromine. The solution may be had of any manufacturing chemist but it is must be quite freshly prepared

The apparatus[*] necessary is figured in the ad-
joining woodcut. It consists of the tube, A, which

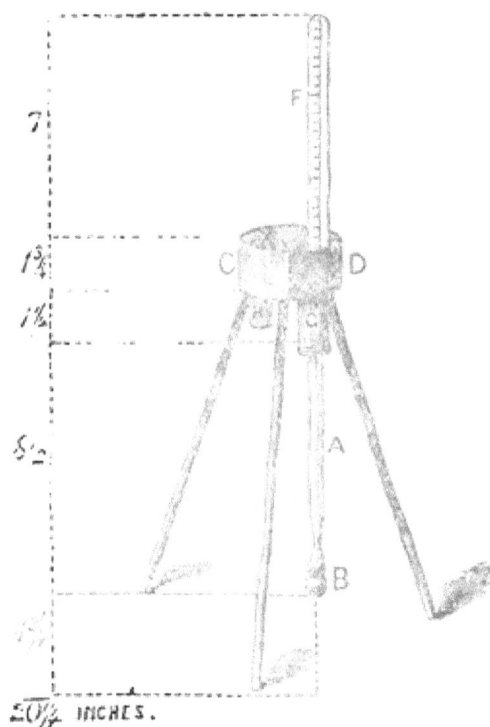

is about 9 inches long, narrowed somewhat before the closed end be reached, which end is
blown out into a bulb, B. The free end is
fitted by means of an india rubber cork into the
hole G at the bottom of the trough C D which

* It may be had of Cetti, Brooke Street, Holborn, price
8s. 6d.

stands on three legs. When an estimation is to be made, 5 C.C. of urine are measured off with a pipette and allowed to run down the side of the tube A, into the bulb B. Distilled water is then added by means of a wash bottle, to wash away the urine adhering to the sides of the tube, but in quantity enough only to fill up the bulb as high as the constriction, or a very little above it. A glass rod tipped with india rubber is then introduced into the tube, A, so that the india rubber fills up the constriction and acts as a cork. Care must be taken that no air bubbles are present below the constriction. The hypobromite solution is then poured into the tube until it be quite full: and the trough filled with common water. The graduated tube F, is then filled with water, the thumb slipped over it, so that it contains no air bubbles, and then inverted in the trough. The glass rod tipped with india rubber is withdrawn, and the graduated tube, F, immediately slipped over the mouth of the tube A. The mouth of this should project well up into the tube F, so as to prevent the escape of any of the gas. The reaction begins immediately, but in order to bring it to an end as quickly as possible, the bulb should be heated

by a spirit lamp or Bunsen's burner till the bulb
be hot to the hand.   In five minutes the amount
of gas may be read off.   After some hours the
gas is lessened in quantity; it is thus important
to read it off as soon as the reaction is over.
The amount of gas measured by the divisions
on the tube gives the percentage of the urea in
the specimen of urine examined.

The estimation of the total amount of urea
excreted in the 24 hours is now easy.   All that
is to be done is to multiply the total number of
cubic centimeters of urine passed by the figures
read off on the measured tube.   Thus, if the
amount of urine passed in the 24 hours be 1770
C.C. and the percentage of the urine 1·8., it is
only necessary to multiply 1770 by 1·8. to get
the amount of urea in milligammes.

This will be 31860 milligrammes, and since
1000 milligrammes equal one gramme, the
total amount of urea passed will be 31·86
grammes.

If the urine contain more than 2 per cent.
of urea, the urine must be diluted with an
equal bulk of distilled water, and the results
doubled.

This method seems likely to be of great value

in clinical research, as it may readily be used in
the wards of a hospital.

The following method is that described by
Liebig.

The solutions required are :

> A standard solution of nitrate of mercury,
> of which 1 C.C. corresponds exactly to
> 10 milligrammes of urea.

> A solution of baryta, made by mixing 2
> volumes of cold saturated solution of
> caustic baryta, with 1 volume of cold
> saturated solution of nitrate of baryta.

> A saturated solution of carbonate of soda.

If the urine be free from albumen, a measured
pipette, containing 10 or 15 C.C., is filled with
urine, *twice,* and the urine allowed to run into a
urine glass or beaker. The same pipette is
next filled with the baryta solution, which is
then added to the urine previously measured off.
There are thus two volumes of urea to one of
baryta solution. The mixture of urine and
baryta is then passed through filtering paper ;
a drop or two of the filtrate is to be tested with
the baryta solution to see if any precipitate
occur, and if any precipitate do occur, it is best
to take a fresh quantity of urine and to add an

equal volume of **baryta solution** ; after **filtration, this** must **again be tested.** The object **of the addition of the baryta is to remove** the phosphates from the urine.

The next step is to measure off a definite quantity of the filtrate, so that in any case it may contain 10 C.C. of urine. Thus, if one volume of baryta solution were used with two volumes of urine, 15 C.C. of the filtrate would be measured off with a pipette. If equal volumes of urine and baryta solution were employed, 20 C.C. must be measured off. A burette divided into quarters of a cubic centimeter is then to be filled with the standard solution of nitrate of mercury. The burette must be filled to the brim, and allowed to remain at rest for some time, so that all bubbles may rise to the surface and burst. The solution must then be let off by the pinch-cock at the bottom of the burette, until the lower of the two black lines, seen by means of transmitted light on the surface of the fluid, be exactly on a level with the first division of the burette. Care must be taken that the solution fills the whole of the apparatus below the pinch-cock, and that no air bubbles are there contained ; for if the latter rise to the surface during the analysis, the estimation is, of course, worthless.

The measured quantity of the filtrate of the urine and baryta is then to be placed in a small glass vessel, a beaker holding about 100 C.C. being best; a few drops of dilute nitric acid are to be added, and the vessel placed under the burette.* The work of estimating the urea now begins. The solution of nitrate of mercury is allowed to run, drop by drop, into the fluid below, stirring the latter well with a glass rod, until a permanent precipitate be produced : the absence, at first, of a permanent precipitate is caused by the chlorides present; the amount of nitrate of mercury used is then read off and

* A great saving of time may be effected by making two separate estimations; in the first estimation, at once adding 15 C.C. of the mercury solution to the fluid in the beaker, testing this with the soda, and then adding the mercury solution in 5 C.C. at a time, and testing with soda after each addition, until a yellow colour is produced. The exact point for the estimation of the urea is found to be between 15 and 20 C.C., or 20 and 25 C.C., as the case may be. A second estimation is then made, and mercury solution to the amount of the smallest number of C.C. *before* the yellow colour was produced, is at once allowed to flow into the beaker, and then added more carefully by quarters or halves of a C.C. as described in the text.

noted down; the nitrate of mercury is then added by quarters or halves of a C.C., the mixture being well stirred after every addition, until a drop of the mixture give a yellow colour when brought into contact with solution of carbonate of soda.

The most convenient method of ascertaining the first appearance of the yellow colour is to place a small glass disc on a piece of black paper, with a few drops of saturated solution of carbonate of soda spread over it; and to let fall as small a drop as possible of the fluid from the beaker into the margin of the soda solution. If no yellow colour be seen, another half C.C. of the mercury solution must be added, and the fluid from the beaker again tested with the soda, and the mercury solution must be added until the least appearance of yellow occur, when one drop more of the mercury solution must be added to the beaker, the fluid well stirred about, and another small drop taken from the mixture and tested with the soda, when, if the process have been rightly performed, an increase in the yellow colour will be perceived. Great care must be taken, during the whole of these operations, not to lose one single drop of the fluid from either the beaker or burette. Then the whole of the carbonate of soda solution contained on the glass plate is to be poured into the beaker, and a drop from this mixture tested with fresh soda; if the yellow colour now appear, the number of C.C. used must be read off; but if not, more of the mercury solution must be dropped into the beaker until the yellow colour appear in the soda, and the number of C.C. used then read off. From the total number of C.C. used, there must be subtracted the number of C.C. used in the first part of the process before a permanent precipitate were produced, and the remainder multiplied by 10 gives the number of milligrammes of urea contained in 10 C.C of urine, because 1 C.C. of the mercury solution corresponds to 10 milligrammes of urea.

Thus far the amount of urea contained in 10 C.C. of urine has been ascertained; by simple proportion it is easy to find the quantity passed in the 24 hours. For example, suppose that 1 C.C. of the mercury solution were used before a permanent precipitate were produced; and that 19 C.C. were used before the yellow colour were distinctly seen, then 1 C.C. subtracted from 19

C.C. leaves **18, which** multiplied by 10 gives **180** milligrammes of urea in **10 C.C.** of urine. Suppose that **the** patient **had passed 1770** C.C. of urine **in the 24 hours, then the calculation would** be as **follows:**

$$10: 1770:: 31860$$
$$180$$

$$10) \overline{318600}$$

31860 milligrammes

As 1000 milligrammes **equal 1 gramme, 31860** milligrammes **equal** 31·860 grammes.

ESTIMATION OF CHLORIDES.

The solutions required are:

- **A standard solution of** nitrate of silver, of **which 1 C.C. corresponds** exactly **to 10 milligrammes of chloride of sodium.**
- A saturated solution of neutral **chromate of** potash.

The urine should be as fresh as possible, and, **if albuminous,** submitted **to the** preparation **described at page 77.** 10 C.C. of urine **are then** measured **off into a glass vessel or beaker,** and

two or three drops of the solution of chromate
of potash added. A burette divided into quarters of a C.C. is then filled with the standard
solution of nitrate of silver, and the precautions
as to filling burettes, described in speaking of
the estimation of urea (page 82) must be observed. The silver solution must then be
allowed to fall into the beaker, and each drop
well mixed with the urine by means of a glass
rod. As each drop falls into the urine, it must
be carefully watched for the least tinge of red
surrounding the precipitate of chloride of silver.
This reddish colour announces the approaching
termination of the process, and is at first not
permanent, but disappears when the fluid in the
beaker is well stirred. The first drop, however,
which produces a reddish tinge, not disappear-
ing by agitation, indicates that the whole of the
chloride present has been precipitated, and that
chromate of silver is beginning to be formed.
The quantity of silver solution used is now read
off, and another drop let fall into the beaker
from the burette, when the reddish colour ought
to be heightened. From the number of C.C.
used, the quantity of chloride is calculated; for,
since 1 C.C. of the silver solution corresponds to

10 milligrammes of chloride of sodium, the
number of C.C. of the silver solution used,
multiplied by 10, will give the amount in milligrammes of the chloride of sodium present in
10 C.C. of urine. Thus if 6 C.C. of silver solution were used before a permanent reddish
precipitate was produced, 10 C.C. of urine will
contain 60 milligrammes of chloride of sodium :
and if the patient passed 1200 C.C. of urine in
the 24 hours, the amount of chloride passed can
be easily calculated in the following way :

$$10 : 1200 : : 60 : 7200.$$

7200 milligrammes equal 7·2 grammes, which
will be the total quantity passed in the 24 hours.

This process, as applied to urine, nearly all-
ways gives results a little above the real amount
present.

For greater accuracy, therefore, 10 C.C. of the
urine are measured off into a porcelain crucible,
1 or 2 grammes of nitrate of potash, free from
chlorides, are dissolved in it, and the whole
slowly evaporated to dryness, and exposed to a
low red heat, until the carbon be completely
oxydised, and the contents of the crucible white.
After cooling, these are dissolved in distilled
water, a few drops of nitric acid added until a

faintly acid reaction be produced, a small quantity of carbonate of lime being then added in order to make the solution again neutral, the solution filtered, and the chlorides then estimated in the manner described above.

ESTIMATION OF PHOSPHATES.

The solutions required are :

A standard solution of acetate of uranium, of which 1 C.C. corresponds exactly to 5 milligrammes of phosphoric acid.

A solution containing acetic acid and acetate of soda : 100 grammes of acetate of soda are dissolved in water, 100 C.C. of acetic acid added, and the mixture diluted until it equal 1000 C.C.

A weak yellowish solution of ferrocyanide of potassium.

50 C.C. of the filtered urine are mixed in a beaker with 5 C.C. of the solution of acetic acid and acetate of soda. The beaker is placed over a water bath, and when the mixture is well warmed, the standard uranium solution is drop-

ped into the beaker until precipitation cease; this can easily be ascertained by allowing the solution to trickle down the side of the beaker. A small drop from the beaker is then to be placed on a porcelain dish by means of a glass rod, and a drop of the solution of ferrocyanide of potassium placed close to it by means of another glass rod, and the two drops allowed to run together. If no alteration of the colour be produced at their line of meeting, more of the uranium solution must be added to the urine, until a drop, tested with the solution of ferrocyanide of potassium, produce a light brown colour where the two fluids meet. The number of C.C. of the uranium solution that have been used is read off; and if, after a second warming of the urine contained in the beaker, and a second trial of the fluid with the solution of the ferrocyanide, no increase in the intensity of the colour be produced, the process may be regarded as completed; but if a dark brown colour be produced by this second trial, too much uranium solution has been added, and the estimation must be begun again with another 50 C.C. of urine.

The calculation for the amount of phosphoric acid passed in 24 hours is now easy.

ESTIMATION OF ALBUMEN.

1 C.C. of uranium solution equals 5 milli-grammes of phosphoric acid. So that, if 15 C.C. of the uranium solution have been used, 50 C.C. of the urine will contain 75 milligrammes of phosphoric acid, and if the patient have passed 1500 C.C. in the 24 hours, the calculation will be

$$50 : 1500 :: 75 : 2250$$
$$\begin{array}{r} 75 \\ 50)112500 \\ \hline 2250 \text{ milligrammes.} \end{array}$$

2250 milligrammes equal 2·25 grammes, which will be the quantity of phosphoric acid passed in the 24 hours.

ESTIMATION OF ALBUMEN.

No easy, rapid, and trustworthy method of estimating the albumen has yet been suggested. The ordinary way of coagulating the albumen by heat and acetic acid, throwing the precipi-tate on a weighed filter, washing, drying, and reweighing, is so long and troublesome that it is never employed in clinical observations.

A fairly good method for clinical observation

is the estimation by means of the polariscope. It is necessary to have the urine moderately transparent, and free from blood-corpuscles, sugar, and bile acids, to obtain results which are tolerably accurate. If the turbidity be persistent after filtration, a few drops of acetic acid, or a little carbonate of soda or milk of lime added to the urine before filtration, may remove the turbidity. For the method of using the polariscope, see page 95.

The quantity of albumen in the urine is usually not more than 1 per cent.; it very rarely rises to 4 per cent. or more. A patient may pass 2 to 20 grms. of albumen in the 24 hours. This latter amount is extreme.

ESTIMATION OF SUGAR.

There are two methods of estimating the amount of sugar present in diabetic urine, either by volumetric analysis, or by means of the polariscope.

Volumetric Method. A standard copper solution is required, containing sulphate of copper, neutral tartrate of soda or potash, and caustic

solution of soda, 20 C.C. of which correspond to
100 milligrammes of grape sugar. This solution is exceedingly apt to decompose, and must
therefore be preserved in well stoppered, completely filled, glass vessels, and in a cool dark
place.

In estimating the sugar, the first step is to
ascertain if the copper solution remain unde-
composed : it may be used in the analysis, if,
after boiling some portion in a test-tube, and
setting it aside for an hour, no precipitate of
copper oxyde have fallen. 20 C.C, of the
copper solution are then measured off with a
pipette, allowed to flow into a glass flask, and
diluted with about 4 times their volume of distilled water. 10 C.C. of the urine are then measured off, and distilled water added until the
mixture exactly measure 100 C.C. If, however,
the urine contain sugar in but small quantity,
it may be diluted with its volume of water only,
or indeed with none at all. A burette is filled
with the diluted urine, and the flask containing
the copper solution is heated over a small flame,
wire gauze intervening, until boiling begin :
2 C.C. of the urine are then allowed to flow into
the boiling copper solution. After a few se-

conds, it must be **carefully noticed if the** copper solution have **lost its** colour, or be still blue. **If** it still appear **blue** when **the flask is** held between **the light and the eye of the observer,** another **C.C. of the urine must be added to the boiling copper solution; then the colour must be noticed, and if it be still blue, the** operation **should be repeated until the colour of** the fluid **have become yellow.** The **analysis is not yet, however, completed.** The **fluid in the flask must be filtered into three test tubes, and to the** first test tube a few drops of the copper **solution must be added, and the whole** boiled to see if an **orange-red** precipitate **of** suboxyde of copper be **produced;** to the second **test tube a small quantity of** hydrochloric acid is added, **and sulphuretted** hydrogen passed through; **to the third, acetic acid and** ferrocyanide of potassium **are added.** None **of these** reagents ought to produce **a precipitate.**

If, on boiling **with the copper solution, a** precipitate occur, too much **urine has** been added; **if, in** either of the two last mentioned test tubes a **precipitate occur,** not enough of the urine has **been added to** decompose all the **copper; in either case, the estimation must be repeated.**

Since 20 C.C. of the copper solution correspond exactly to 100 milligrammes of sugar, the complete decoloration of the copper solution will be accomplished by exactly 100 milligrammes of sugar. If, therefore, for the 20 C.C. of copper, 15·5 C.C. of the dilute urine were required for complete removal of colour, and if the dilute urine contained only 10 per cent. of urine, 1·55 C.C. of urine will contain 100 milligrammes of sugar, and 100 C.C. of urine will contain 6·45 grm. of sugar ; as by proportion :

$$1\cdot55 : 100 : : 100 : 6450.$$

If the urine contain albumen as well as sugar, the former must be removed as directed, page 77.

Estimation by means of the Polariscope. By means of this instrument an estimation of the sugar present can be made, provided that the urine be moderately transparent. If it be passed through animal charcoal, the accuracy is greater of course, but not so great as to be of much consequence in purely clinical research. If the urine contain albumen, it must be removed by the method given above, page 77. The bile acids, when present, can scarcely affect the result, since they are found in such very small amount in the urine.

The polariscope consists of a tube, supported upon a foot, and divided into three parts, one of which, the middle, is moveable, but the other two, which are at the ends of the instrument, are fixed. One of the fixed tubes is furnished with a small screw, attached to its lower surface; this may be called the eye-piece. The other fixed tube has no screw attached to it; it may be called the object-glass.

A good argand burner, or a gas lamp, protected by a neutral tinted glass cylinder, is necessary. When the polariscope is to be used, the lamp is placed an inch or so in front of the object-glass. The hollow glass tube in the middle of the instrument must now be removed, and filled with distilled water; the small glass disc being slid over the end of the tube completely filled with water, in such a manner that no air-bubbles are included in the tubes; the metal cover to keep the glass disc in its place is then attached to the tube, and the tube freed carefully from all moisture. The tube is now set in its place in the middle of the instrument; and the observer, looking through the eye-piece, draws out, or pushes in, the moveable tube close to the eye, until he see at the end of the eye-piece, nearer to the lamp, a circular field divided into two equal parts by a black line, which ought to be sufficiently well defined. He next turns the screw attached to the under surface of the eye-piece to the right or left, as may be required, until the colour of the two halves of the field be exactly the same. The observer then notices whether the zeroes on the scale above the eye-piece be exactly opposite to each other. If they be not, the little button at the end of the scale should be gently turned, until they quite coincide.

Before adjusting the instrument, the urine may be set aside to filter, or to pass through animal charcoal, if that be at hand. If the fluid be as free from colour as ordinary diabetic urine, it may be observed in the longer tube, 20 centimeters in length, since the accuracy of the estimation is increased with the length of the tube. But if the fluid be dark, the shorter tube, 10 centimeters long must be used.

The tube is now filled with the urine, in the same manner as it was previously filled with distilled water, and again placed in the middle of the instrument. The observer then notices if any alteration in colour of the two halves of the field have taken place. If the uniformity of colour no longer exist, he should turn the screw below the eye-piece until the two halves of the field appear of precisely the same tint. The eyes are best rested occasionally during this part of the operation by looking on some white surface, as the ceiling of the room, or a sheet of paper. When the two semi-circles become exactly the same in colour, the number of degrees which the moveable zero is distant from the fixed zero is read off; and if the fluid observed contain sugar, the moveable scale will be found to the right: but if the albumen only, to the left. The number of degrees that the zero has moved gives, when divided by 2, the percentage amount of either sugar or albumen, if the longer tube were used; but the percentage is at once known, if the shorter tube were employed, as it is the same in amount with the number of degrees by which two zeroes are separated from each other.

INDEX.

NEW BOOKS

Published by

H. K. LEWIS, 136 GOWER STREET, LONDON.

A Handbook of the Theory and Practice of
MEDICINE. *By F. T. ROBERTS, M.D., B.Sc., Assistant Physician
and Teacher of Clinical Medicine in the University College Hospital;
Assistant Physician, Brompton Consumption Hospital, &c. Second
edition, demy 8vo, cloth,* 18s.

A Handbook of Therapeutics. By Sydney
RINGER, *M.D., Professor of Therapeutics in University College,
Fifth edition, demy 8vo, cloth,* 12s. 6d.

The Diseases of the Nose and its Accessory
CAVITIES. *By W. SPENCER WATSON, F.R.C.S. Eng., B.M.
Lond., Surgeon to the Great Northern Hospital; Surgeon to the Royal
South London Ophthalmic Hospital, and to the Central London Oph-
thalmic Hospital; formerly Assistant Surgeon to King's College Hospi-
tal. Profusely illustrated, demy 8vo, cloth,* 18s.

A Text-Book of Human Physiology; Designed
*for the use of Practitioners and Students of Medicine. By AUSTIN
FLINT, Jun., M.D., Professor of Physiology and Physiological Anatomy in the Bellevue Hospital Medical College, New York, &c. Large
8vo, copiously illustrated by plates and wood engravings,* 28s.

A Treatise on the Diseases of the Nervous
SYSTEM. *By WILLIAM A. HAMMOND, M.D., Professor of Diseases of the Mind and Nervous System, University of New York, &c.,
&c. Sixth edition, rewritten, enlarged and improved, illustrated, large
8vo,* 25s.

A Treatise on the Diseases of Infancy and
CHILDHOOD. *By J. LEWIS SMITH, M.D., Consulting Physician
to the class of Children's Diseases, Out-door Department of Bellevue
Hospital; Clinical Lecturer on Diseases of Children in Bellevue Hospital Medical College. Third edition, enlarged and thoroughly revised
with illustrations, large 8vo,* 24s.

On Extra-Uterine Pregnancy; its Clinical His-
TORY, DIAGNOSIS, PROGNOSIS AND TREATMENT. By
JOHN S. PARRY, M.D., Obstetrician to the Philadelphia Hospital;
Vice-President of the Obstetrical Society of Philadelphia. Illustra-
tions, large 8vo, cloth, 8s.

The Heart and its Diseases: with their Treat-
MENT. By J. M. FOTHERGILL, M.D., M.R.C.P., Junior Physician to the West London Hospital. 8vo, 12s 6d.

Affections of the Heart, and in its Neighbour-
HOOD. CASES, APHORISMS, AND COMMENTARIES. By
HORACE DOBELL, M.D. Senior Physician to the Royal Hospital for Diseases of the Chest, &c. Illustrated by the Heliotype process. 8vo, cloth, 6s. 6d. [Reprint].

On the Temperature of the Body as a means
OF DIAGNOSIS AND PROGNOSIS IN PHTHISIS. By SYDNEY
RINGER, M.D., Professor of Therapeutics in University College.
Second edition, small 8vo, cloth, 2s. 6d.

The Science and Practice of Medicine in Rela-
TION TO MIND, THE PATHOLOGY OF NERVE CENTRES,
AND THE JURISPRUDENCE OF INSANITY: being a course of
lectures delivered at Guy's Hospital. By J. THOMPSON DICKSON,
M.A., M.B. Cantab., Lecturer on Mental Diseases at Guy's Hospital;
late Superintendent at St. Luke's Hospital. Illustrations in chromo-
lithography and physiognomical portraits, 8vo, cloth, 14s.

Outlines of Pictorial Diagnosis Of Diseases of
WOMEN. By Dr. GRAILY HEWITT, Professor of Midwifery and
Diseases of Women in University College. 4to, 6s.

A Text-book of Practical Medicine, with par-
ticular reference to Physiology and Pathological Anatomy. By FELIX
VON NIEMEYER. Translated from the eighth German edition, by
special permission of the Author, by GEORGE H. HUMPHREY,
M.D., and CHARLES E. HACKLEY, M.D. 2 vols., large 8vo, 36s.

www.ingramcontent.com/pod-product-compliance
Lightning Source LLC
Chambersburg PA
CBHW030540270326
41927CB00008B/1453